Clay Creations For All

Turn colorful clay into fun or fancy gifts and accessories! This book introduces the basic techniques and gives step-by-step instructions for each project.

2

4

8

10

12

16

18

20

LEISURE ARTS, INC. • Maumelle, Arkansas

BLUE BIRD

Designed by Britta Launtenschlager for Polyform Products

Finished Size: about 2$^{1}/_{4}$" wide x 4" long x 2" tall

SHOPPING LIST

- ☐ Sculpey® III Oven Bake Clay 2 oz. - 1 bar each of Jewelry Gold and Black; 2 bars of Tranquility
- ☐ Sculpey® Clay Conditioning Machine
- ☐ Sculpey® Acrylic Roller
- ☐ Sculpey® Flexible Texture Sheets - Landscape
- ☐ mica powder - gold
- ☐ spray water bottle
- ☐ wax paper, aluminum foil, clay dedicated metal baking sheet, or Sculpey® Work 'n Bake Clay Mat for work surface
- ☐ tape (optional)
- ☐ glass baking dish, metal pan, or cookie sheet covered with an index card for small projects or parchment paper or aluminum foil for large projects
- ☐ oven thermometer

To make the Blue Bird:

Preheat oven to 275°F. Read ***General Instructions****, pages 23-24, before beginning.*

1. Condition the Tranquility clay on the #3 setting. For the wings, make two $^{7}/_{8}$" diameter balls and shape them into flattened teardrop shapes ***(Fig. 1)***; set aside.

Fig. 1

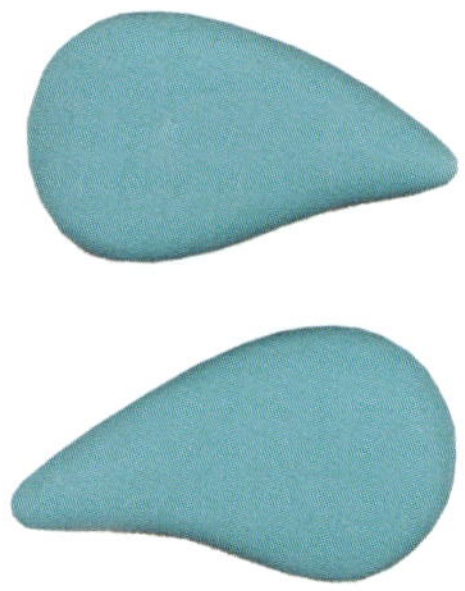

2. Shape the rest of the clay into the bird's body, head, and tail feathers. Lightly mist the tail feathers with water and press the floral texture sheet into the tail feathers.
3. Press the wings to the sides of the body. Lightly mist the wings with water and press the floral texture sheet into the wings.
4. Dip your finger in the mica powder and lightly spread it on the texture on the tail feathers and wings.
5. Shape a small Jewelry Gold beak and two tiny Black eyes ***(Fig. 2)***. Press the beak and eyes onto the head.

Fig. 2

6. Follow the manufacturer's instructions to bake the bird.

LAURA MORIARTY
The REST
TRACY CHEVALIER
REMARKABL

GREETING CARD

Designed by Iris Weiss for Polyform Products.

Finished Size: 4$^{1}/_{4}$" x 6"

SHOPPING LIST

- ☐ premo! Sculpey® Oven Bake Clay 2 oz. - Jungle
- ☐ Sculpey® Clay Conditioning Machine
- ☐ Sculpey® Acrylic Roller
- ☐ Sculpey® Clay Tool Starter Set
- ☐ scrapbook paper - green print, brown print (Our green print paper is two-sided.)
- ☐ kraft paper tag for sentiment (Ours is 2$^{1}/_{8}$" x 3$^{5}/_{8}$".)
- ☐ scrap of paper for stencil
- ☐ rubber stamp with sentiment (We used Tim Holtz® Stamper's Anonymous Cling Mounted Rubber Stamp Set - Stuff to Say CMS110)
- ☐ rubber stamp - random texture
- ☐ brown dye ink stamp pad (We used Tsukineko® Memento™ Dew Drop Fade Resistant Dye Ink in Rich Cocoa.)
- ☐ green chalk pigma ink stamp pad (We used Tsukineko® Versa Magic™ Dew Drop Chalk Pigma Ink in Hint of Pesto.)
- ☐ Jacquard® PearlEx Powdered Pigment - Interference Green
- ☐ pressed ginkgo leaf (Can be purchased at www.naturespressed.com.)
- ☐ bakers twine - natural/copper
- ☐ Scotch® Quick-Dry Adhesive
- ☐ Elmer's® Glue-All™ multi-purpose glue
- ☐ white bathroom tissue, separate to have one ply
- ☐ sponge paintbrush
- ☐ small piece of wax paper
- ☐ aluminum foil
- ☐ tape
- ☐ glass baking dish, metal pan, or cookie sheet covered with an index card for small projects or parchment paper or aluminum foil for large projects
- ☐ oven thermometer
- ☐ craft knife

Life
IS WHAT
HAPPENS
TO US
WHILE WE
ARE MAKING
OTHER
PLANS
PERSUASION
JANE AUSTEN

To make the Card:

*Preheat oven to 275°F. Read **General Instructions**, pages 23-24, before beginning.*

Making the Clay Leaves

1. Condition the clay on the #3 setting ***(Fig. 1)***.

Fig. 1

2. To make a stencil, trace the leaf pattern on the scrap paper; cut out the leaf. Use the stencil and a craft knife to cut two leaves from the sheet of clay ***(Fig. 2)***.

Fig. 2

3. Turn one leaf over. Using the pointed tool, add vein lines to the leaves ***(Fig. 3)***. Be careful not to cut through the leaf. Press the edges of the leaves slightly thinner.

Fig. 3

4. To highlight the leaves, use your finger to apply the green powdered pigment randomly. Position the leaves on the index card, adding shaping, high and low areas, curls and twists ***(Fig. 4)***. Follow the manufacturer's instructions to bake the leaves; cool completely. Set the leaves aside. Do not turn off the oven.

Fig. 4

Making the Sealed Ginkgo Leaf

1. Place a piece of aluminum foil on the baking dish, metal pan, or cookie sheet.

2. Place the wax paper on the foil. Place the pressed ginkgo leaf on the wax paper. Cover the leaf with one ply of bathroom tissue.

3. Thoroughly mix about $^{1}/_{4}$ cup of Elmer's glue with two tablespoons of water. Using the sponge paintbrush, carefully apply a coat of the thinned Elmer's glue on top of the tissue. Bake for 10 minutes. Remove from oven and allow to cool.

4. Remove the ginkgo leaf from the foil. Tear a square around the leaf ***(Fig. 5)***. Using the green stamp pad and the texture stamp, randomly stamp on the tissue paper side of the sealed leaf. Ink the edges of the sealed leaf with the brown stamp pad.

Fig. 5

Making the Tag

1. Ink the edges of the tag with the brown stamp pad.

2. Use the brown stamp pad to stamp the sentiment on the tag close to the bottom; set aside.

Making the Card

1. Trim the green print paper to $8^1/_2$" x 6". Fold paper in half to create a card that is $4^1/_4$" x 6". Trim the brown scrapbook paper to $^5/_8$" x $4^1/_4$". Ink the edges of both pieces with the brown stamp pad.

2. Use the quick-dry adhesive to adhere the brown strip to the front of the card $1^1/_8$" from the bottom; set aside.

3. Cut two 6" pieces of the twine. Holding the lengths together, loop them through the tag and trim the ends as desired. Arrange the 2 clay ginkgo leaves coming out of the hole in the tag. If necessary, you can trim the tops of the leaves with the craft knife so they fit nicely. Adhere the leaves to the tag with the quick-dry adhesive.

4. Using the quick-dry adhesive, adhere the sealed ginkgo leaf and the tag to the card.

SWITCH PLATE

Designed by Gretchen Amberg for Polyform Products

SHOPPING LIST

- ☐ Sculpey® Soufflé Oven Bake Clay 1.7 oz. - Cowboy
- ☐ Sculpey® Clay Conditioning Machine
- ☐ Sculpey® Acrylic Roller
- ☐ Sculpey® Super Slicer
- ☐ Sculpey® Flexible Texture Sheets - Edgy
- ☐ Sculpey® Wet/Dry Sand Paper Variety Pack
- ☐ Sculpey® Satin Glaze or Gloss Glaze
- ☐ paintbrush (optional)
- ☐ metal switch plate
- ☐ gold leaf
- ☐ spray water bottle
- ☐ craft knife
- ☐ wax paper, aluminum foil, clay dedicated metal baking sheet, or Sculpey® Work 'n Bake Clay Mat for work surface
- ☐ tape (optional)
- ☐ glass baking dish, metal pan, or cookie sheet covered with an index card for small projects or parchment paper or aluminum foil for large projects
- ☐ oven thermometer
- ☐ Super Glue®

To make the Cover:

*Preheat oven to 275°F. Read **General Instructions**, pages 23-24, before beginning.*

1. Condition the clay on the #2 setting. Make sure the sheet is large enough to cover the switch plate with at least 1/2" extra on all sides.
2. Very carefully place a sheet of the gold leaf on the surface of the clay sheet; don't worry too much about any places where it creases. Use your fingers to smooth the gold leaf onto the clay. If you have any spots that aren't covered or where there is a tear, place small pieces of gold leaf on top and smooth it down.
3. The copper ceiling texture is part of a large sheet of different textures. Cutting on the line between the patterns, cut the copper ceiling texture apart from the remaining textures.

4. Lightly mist the clay with water. Starting at the top corner, press the texture sheet into the clay until you get a deep, complete impression. Lift the sheet and move it to another area, continuing the impression you just made. Make sure the edges connect to create the complete pattern ***(Fig. 1)***. Continue until you have the entire sheet covered.

Fig. 1

5. Lay the patterned sheet of clay on top of the switch plate. Make sure the pattern is square with the switch plate. Gently smooth the clay onto the surface, making sure it conforms to any slopes and curves. Turn the plate over and use the Super Slicer to trim the excess clay from the edges. Use the craft knife to make the holes for the screws. Cutting from the back, use the craft knife to cut the clay out of the hole for the switch.

6. Follow the manufacturer's instructions to bake; allow to cool.

7. Wet a piece of 400 grit sandpaper. Gently sand the switch plate to remove the gold leaf from the raised areas while leaving it in the impressions ***(Fig. 2)***. Use the 400 grit sandpaper until you have most of the gold leaf sanded off. Repeat this process with the 600 grit and then the 800 grit until you have the raised areas completely clear of gold leaf and nice and smooth.

Fig. 2

8. Apply a thin coat of Glaze over the sanded clay; allow to dry.

9. Gently pry the clay off the switch plate. Add a small dot of Super Glue in each corner. Press the clay back on the plate and let the glue set. Attach the switch plate to the wall.

CUPCAKE CHARM BRACELET

Finished Size: about 7" long

SHOPPING LIST

- ☐ Sculpey® III Oven Bake Clay 2 oz. - Emerald and other desired colors
- ☐ Sculpey® Clay Tool Starter Set
- ☐ silver chain bracelet
- ☐ eye pins
- ☐ jump rings
- ☐ chain-nose pliers (2 pair)
- ☐ wire cutters
- ☐ craft glue
- ☐ wax paper, aluminum foil, clay dedicated metal baking sheet, or Sculpey® Work 'n Bake Clay Mat for work surface
- ☐ tape (optional)
- ☐ glass baking dish, metal pan, or cookie sheet covered with an index card for small projects or parchment paper or aluminum foil for large projects
- ☐ oven thermometer

To make the Bracelet:

*Preheat oven to 275°F. Read **General Instructions**, pages 23-24, before beginning.*

1. Hand condition small portions of each color of the clay.

2. For the cupcake cup, roll a $^{1}/_{2}$" ball of desired color. Flatten two sides of the ball. Use the Sculpey tool to make lines on the sides.

3. Roll a $^{1}/_{4}$" ball of any color; place the ball on top of the cup. For the icing, roll a very thin rope of desired color; coil the rope on top, covering the ball.

4. For the flowers, roll tiny ball(s) of desired color; press the flowers onto the icing. For the leaf, roll a very tiny ball of emerald. Flatten the ball and shape into a leaf; press the leaf onto the icing.

5. Trim an eye pin to about $^{3}/_{8}$". Push the eye pin into the cupcake.

6. Repeat Steps 2-5 to make as many cupcakes as desired.

7. Follow the manufacturer's instructions to bake the cupcakes.

8. After baking, place a small drop of glue where each eye pin is inserted. Use the chain-nose pliers to attach a jump ring to each eye pin and to attach the jump ring to the bracelet.

Opening and Closing Jump Rings

Pick up a jump ring with chain-nose pliers. With a second pair of chain-nose pliers, gently hold the other side of the ring. Open the ring by pulling one pair of pliers toward you while pushing the other away ***(Fig. 1)***.

Fig. 1

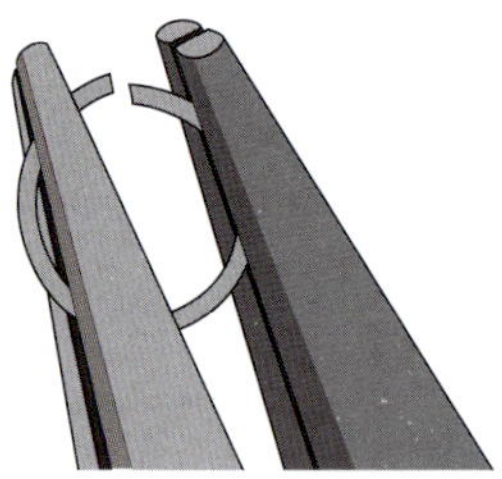

Close the ring by pushing and pulling the pliers in opposite directions, bringing the ring ends back together.

DIAMOND MOSAIC FRAME

Designed by Amy Koranek for Polyform Products

SHOPPING LIST

- ☐ 8" x 8" wood frame with 3 1/2" x 3 1/2" opening
- ☐ Sculpey® III Oven Bake Clay 2 oz. - Suede Brown, Camouflage, Buried Treasure, Silver, and Tranquility
- ☐ Translucent Liquid Sculpey® bakeable transfer and color medium
- ☐ Sculpey® Clay Conditioning Machine
- ☐ Sculpey® Acrylic Roller
- ☐ premo! Sculpey® Diamond Metal Cutters
- ☐ Sculpey® Flexible Texture Sheets - Landscape and Edgy
- ☐ Sculpey® Texture Wheel
- ☐ Sculpey® Texture Wheel Head Pack (includes Greek Key, Argyle, Whirl, and Wrought Iron)
- ☐ Sculpey® Super Slicer
- ☐ mica powder - antique silver
- ☐ silver ball chain
- ☐ silver beads
- ☐ assorted small metal grommets
- ☐ metal scrapbooking elements
- ☐ acrylic paint that coordinates with clay colors for painting the wood frame
- ☐ paintbrush
- ☐ sandpaper
- ☐ spray water bottle
- ☐ paper towels
- ☐ wax paper, aluminum foil, clay dedicated metal baking sheet, or Sculpey® Work 'n Bake Clay Mat for work surface
- ☐ tape (optional)
- ☐ glass baking dish, metal pan, or cookie sheet covered with an index card for small projects or parchment paper or aluminum foil for large projects
- ☐ oven thermometer
- ☐ Super Glue® (optional)
- ☐ cardstock (optional)

togetherness

To make the Frame:

Preheat oven to 275°F. Read ***General Instructions****, pages 23-24, before beginning.*

Preparing the Frame

1. Sand the wood frame.

2. Paint the inside and outside edges of the frame; allow to dry.

Texturing the Clay

1. The texture is either a single sheet or a part of a sheet of different textures. If the texture you are using is part of a sheet of different textures, cut on the line between the patterns to cut the desired texture apart from the remaining textures.

2. Condition the Camouflage clay on the #1 setting. Spritz the clay lightly with water. Starting at the top corner, press the paver brick texture sheet into the clay until you get a full, deep impression. Lift the sheet and move it to another area, continuing the impression you just made. Make sure the edges connect to create the complete pattern. Continue until you have the entire sheet covered ***(Fig. 1)***. Blot excess water with a paper towel.

Fig. 1

3. Repeat Step 2 using the Tranquility clay and the snakeskin texture sheet ***(Fig. 2)***.

Fig. 2

4. Repeat Step 2 using the Buried Treasure clay and the fishnet texture sheet ***(Fig. 3)***.

Fig. 3

5. Condition the Suede Brown clay on the #1 setting. Use the Greek Key texture wheel to make straight parallel lines of texture in the clay. Dip your finger in the mica powder and spread it on the textured clay ***(Fig. 4)***.

Fig. 4

6. Condition the Silver clay on the #1 setting. Fold it so it is double thickness. You will want the shape of this piece to be long and narrow. Texture the sheet along the length with the argyle texture wheel. Use the Super Slicer to cut apart the argyle texture in long strips ***(Fig. 5)***. These strips will be used as borders between the diamond shapes.

Fig. 5

Covering the Frame Front

Note: *You will want to see how your diamond-shaped pieces will lay out on the frame. You can either lay them directly on the wood frame to see how they fit or you can make a cardstock template of your frame to work on.*

1. Starting with the largest size of diamond cutters, cut out a few diamonds from each textured clay sheet. Start in one corner of your frame or template and lay the diamonds side by side from top corner to inside corner. Border the diamonds with strips of the Silver argyle ***(Fig. 6)***.

Fig. 6

2. Working your way around the frame, continue cutting out various sized diamonds and placing them in patterns. Use the Silver argyle strips to fill in gaps and to make the patterns connect. You can also slice the argyles in half lengthwise to fill spaces ***(Fig. 7)***.

Fig. 7

3. Once you have planned the pattern for the entire frame, remove all the pieces and set them aside in the same arrangement. Cover the front of the frame with a thin layer of Translucent Liquid Sculpey. Replace the clay pieces on the frame. Trim around both the inside and outside edges so that the clay pieces align with the frame edges.

4. Use ball chain as a decorative element along some of the edges of the Silver argyle strips as desired. Imbed the ball chain in the clay so that the clay holds it in place.

5. Cut a few of the smallest diamonds from each textured clay sheet. Lay them over the base diamonds as decorative elements. Press a metal grommet in the center of these small diamonds.

6. Press silver beads into the clay as desired. If desired, add a ball of clay behind the bead to hold it in place.

7. Use Super Glue to add a metal word tag or other metal scrapbook elements to your frame.

8. Follow the manufacturer's instructions to bake the frame and the clay. Baking the wood frame may cause some sap or glue to leak out between the wood fibers. If this happens, allow the frame to cool completely and then remove the sap and/or glue with sandpaper. Touch up the paint, if needed, before displaying the frame.

INK PEN

Designed by Patricia Kimle Designs for Polyform Products

SHOPPING LIST

- ☐ Sculpey® Soufflé Oven Bake Clay 1.7 oz - Poppy Seed, Canary, Igloo, Pistachio, Jade, Robin's Egg, Lagoon, Pumpkin, So 80's, Cherry Pie, and Royalty
- ☐ Sculpey® Clay Conditioning Machine
- ☐ Sculpey® Super Slicer
- ☐ Sculpey® Acrylic Roller
- ☐ Bic® Round Stic® pen
- ☐ tape (optional)
- ☐ wax paper, aluminum foil, clay dedicated metal baking sheet, or Sculpey® Work 'n Bake Clay Mat for work surface
- ☐ glass baking dish, metal pan, or cookie sheet covered with an index card for small projects or parchment paper or aluminum foil for large projects
- ☐ oven thermometer

To make the Pen:

*Preheat oven to 275°F. Read **General Instructions**, pages 23-24, before beginning.*

1. Condition about 1/4 of the package of the Poppy Seed clay on the #3 setting. Roll at #6 on the clay conditioning machine to a sheet about 2" x 8".

2. Condition each additional color. Roll a rope about 1/8" diameter and about 4" long ***(Fig. 1)***. Cut each rope in half.

Fig. 1

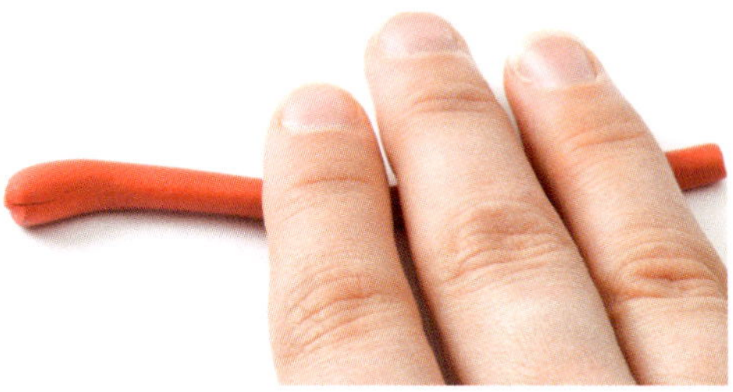

3. Arrange the ropes of clay along the Poppy Seed sheet as desired, leaving at least 1/8" between each color ***(Fig. 2)***. Repeat the arrangement again to fill the length of the sheet.

Fig. 2

4. Loosely roll up the sheet into a log-shaped cane so that the spacing between the colors remains ***(Fig. 3)***.

Fig. 3

5. Working from the center outward, compress the cane with your hands ***(Fig. 4)***, working the air out and letting the Poppy Seed fill in a bit between the colors. Reduce the cane to about 3/8" diameter.

Fig. 4

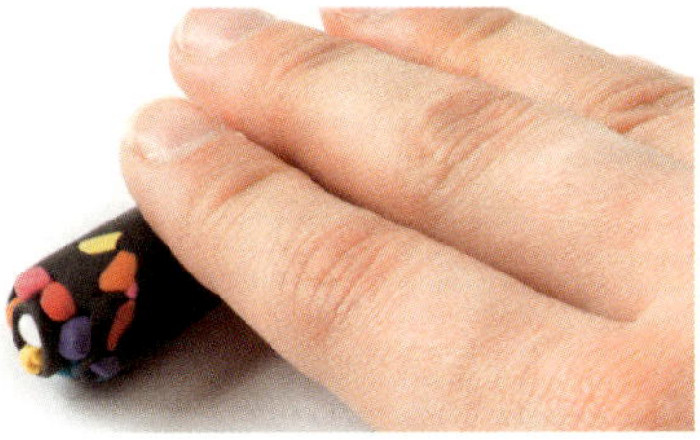

6. Remove the cartridge from the ink pen. Roll another sheet of Poppy Seed at #6 on the clay conditioning machine to a sheet about $1\frac{1}{2}$" wide and the length of the pen barrel.

7. Sawing back and forth so that the cane does not "squish," use the Super Slicer to cut slices from the cane as thin as possible and arrange them closely on the clay sheet ***(Fig. 5)***.

Fig. 5

8. Use the acrylic roller to roll across the sheet to compress the slices into the clay sheet ***(Fig. 6)***.

Fig. 6

9. Run the sheet through the conditioning machine at #7.

10. Trim one long edge of the sheet straight and align it along the pen barrel. Wrap the sheet smoothly around the pen barrel ***(Fig. 7)***, being careful not to trap any air between the sheet and the barrel. Trim the other side of the sheet so the long edges just meet. Blend the seam together with your fingers.

Fig. 7

11. Trim the clay even with the ink cartridge opening of the pen. Smooth the ends of the clay closed around the top of the pen barrel.

12. Follow the manufacturer's instructions to bake; allow to cool. Insert the ink cartridge in the pen.

BEE & LADYBUG

Finished Size: about 2" wide x 1$^3/_4$" tall (excluding antennae)

SHOPPING LIST

- ☐ Sculpey® III Oven Bake Clay 2 oz. - Yellow, Red Hot Red, Black, Blue, and White
- ☐ Sculpey® Clay Tool Starter Set
- ☐ 22-gauge black wire
- ☐ $^3/_4$" magnetic button with foam adhesive
- ☐ wax paper, aluminum foil, clay dedicated metal baking sheet, or Sculpey® Work 'n Bake Clay Mat for work surface
- ☐ tape (optional)
- ☐ craft glue
- ☐ oven thermometer
- ☐ glass baking dish, metal pan, or cookie sheet covered with an index card for small projects or parchment paper or aluminum foil for large projects

To make the Bee:

*Preheat oven to 275°F. Read **General Instructions**, pages 23-24, before beginning.*

1. Hand condition Yellow, Red Hot Red, Black, and White clay.
2. For the body, roll a $^3/_4$" ball of Yellow; shape it into a flattened oval.
3. For the stripes, roll two very thin ropes of Black. Lay the ropes across the body and press them down slightly.
4. For the head, roll a $^5/_8$" ball of Yellow. Shape the ball into a head; press the head onto the body.
5. For the eyes, roll two very tiny balls of Black; press them onto the head.
6. For the nose, roll a tiny ball of Red Hot Red; press it onto the head.
7. Use the Sculpey tool to make a smile.
8. For the antennae, cut two $^5/_8$" pieces of wire. Roll two tiny balls of Black. Press the balls on the ends of the wires and the wires into the head.
9. For the arms, roll two $^3/_8$" balls of Black. Shape the balls into arms; press the arms onto the body.
10. For the feet, roll two $^1/_4$" balls of Black. Flatten the balls to shape into feet; press the feet onto the body.
11. For the wings, roll two $^1/_2$" balls of White. Flatten the balls into ovals for wings; press the wings onto the body ***(Fig. 1)***.

Fig. 1

12. Follow the manufacturer's instructions to bake the bee.
13. After baking, place a small drop of glue where each wire is inserted. Attach the magnet to the back.

To make the Ladybug:

*Preheat oven to 275°F. Read **General Instructions**, pages 23-24, before beginning.*

1. Hand condition small portions of Red Hot Red, Black, Blue, and White clay.

2. For the body, roll a 1" ball of Red Hot Red. Use the Sculpey tool to make a line on the body.

3. For the spots, roll tiny Black balls; press the spots onto the body.

4. For the head, roll a $^1/_2$" ball of Black; press the head onto the body.

5. For the eyes, roll two small balls of White and two tiny balls of Blue. Press the Blue balls into the White balls; press the eyes onto the head.

6. For the mouth, roll a very tiny ball of Red Hot Red; press the mouth onto the head.

7. For the antennae, cut two $^5/_8$" pieces of wire. Roll two tiny balls of Black. Press the balls on the ends of the wires and the wires into the head.

8. Follow the manufacturer's instructions to bake the ladybug.

9. After baking, place a small drop of glue where each wire is inserted. Attach the magnet to the back.

COVERED MINT TIN

Designed by Britta Launtenschlager for Polyform Products

SHOPPING LIST

- ☐ Sculpey® Soufflé Oven Bake Clay 1.7 oz - 1 bar each of Igloo, Pumpkin, and Canary; 2 bars each of Robin's Egg and Lagoon
- ☐ small mint tin
- ☐ Sculpey® Clay Conditioning Machine
- ☐ Sculpey® Acrylic Clay Roller
- ☐ Sculpey® Super Slicer
- ☐ Sculpey® Bake & Bond
- ☐ Sculpey® Wet/Dry Sand Paper
- ☐ Sculpey® Style & Detail Tools
- ☐ wax paper, aluminum foil, clay dedicated metal baking sheet, or Sculpey® Work 'n Bake Clay Mat for work surface
- ☐ tape (optional)
- ☐ glass baking dish, metal pan, or cookie sheet covered with an index card for small projects or parchment paper or aluminum foil for large projects
- ☐ oven thermometer
- ☐ soft cloth
- ☐ rough sandpaper for texturing
- ☐ scrap of paper

To make the Tin:

*Preheat oven to 275°F. Read **General Instructions**, pages 23-24, before beginning.*

Conditioning the Clay

1. Condition 1 bar each of the Igloo, Robin's Egg, Pumpkin, and Lagoon clays on the #1 setting. Always work lightest color to darkest color.

2. Condition 1 bar of the Canary clay on the #3 setting.

Making the Striped Rim

1. Stack Pumpkin, Robin's Egg, and Canary together and run them through the clay conditioning machine on the #1 setting.

2. Stack Lagoon and Igloo together and run them through the clay conditioning machine on the #1 setting.

3. Stack sheets from Steps 1 and 2 together with Canary and Lagoon in the middle and run them through the clay conditioning machine on the #1 setting.

4. Cut the stacked sheet in half. You will use one half for the striped rim and one half for the mokume gane lid.

5. For the striped rim, use one of the halves from Step 4, above, and cut the sheet in half; stack one half on top of the other. Repeat this step three more times to create a tall stack of clay. Trim one tall side straight.

6. Lay the stack down on the straight side. Slice thin strips of the stack ***(Fig. 1)***.

Fig. 1

7. Spread a thin layer of Bake & Bond on the sides of the tin bottom. With the tin closed, align the strips with the lid and press the strips end to end around the tin bottom. Cut off any excess clay along the bottom edge. Open the tin all the way to press down any clay that is in the way of the hinges.

Making the Mokume Gane Lid

1. To make the mokume gane lid, take the remaining half from Step 4, above, and cut and stack the sheet of clay. Repeat two more times to create a short rectangle.

2. Using two different size Style & Detail ball tools, randomly press them into the clay. Make sure you press deeply so that when you slice off the layers the pattern will be on all slices. With the Super Slicer, cut off slices of the stack ***(Fig. 2)*** and choose one for your lid; set aside.

Fig. 2

3. Condition the remaining bar of Robin's Egg clay on the #3 setting ***(Fig. 3)***.

Fig. 3

4. For the top and bottom of the tin, place the tin on top of the clay sheet and cut around it twice using a craft knife ***(Fig. 4)***.

Fig. 4

5. Apply Bake & Bond on the top of the tin. Press the cutout piece on the top of the tin and smooth the edges. Repeat with the remaining piece on the bottom of the tin. With the sandpaper, press a rough texture into the top and bottom ***(Fig. 5)***.

Fig. 5

6. Press the slice of Mokume Gane on the top of the clay-covered tin; smooth the edges ***(Fig. 6)***. Follow the manufacturer's instructions to bake; allow to cool.

Fig. 6

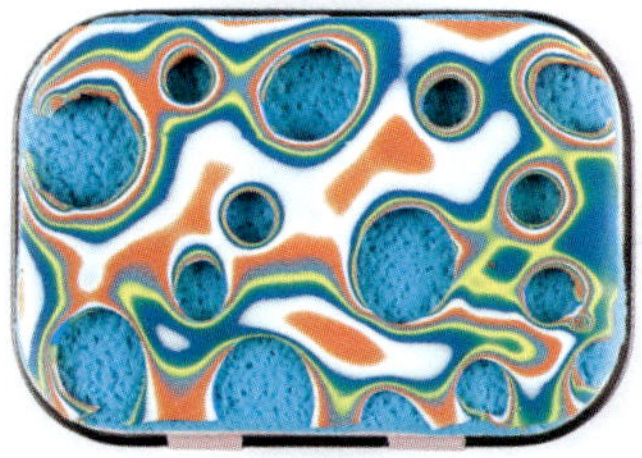

7. Condition the remaining bar of Lagoon clay on the #2 setting. Using the Super Slicer, cut a long thin strip slightly wider than the upper rim of the tin ***(Fig. 7)***. Apply Bake & Bond on the sides of the tin lid; press the strip to the tin.

Fig. 7

8. With the sandpaper, press a rough texture into the clay rim. Cut off any excess clay above and below the rim. Open the tin all the way, to press down any clay that is in the way of the hinges. Follow the manufacturer's instructions to bake the tin; allow to cool.

Completing the Tin

1. For the legs, make four $^1/_2$" diameter balls from Lagoon clay ***(Fig. 8)***; press the balls to the bottom of the tin. Follow the manufacturer's instructions to bake the tin; allow to cool.

Fig. 8

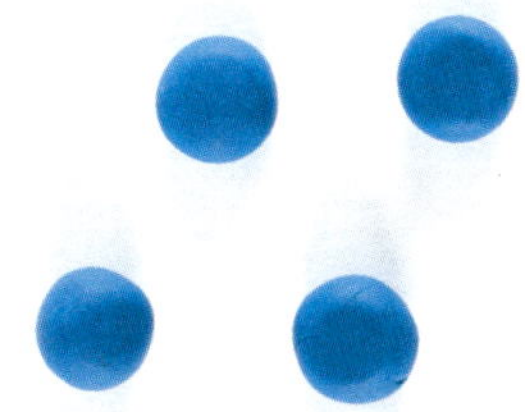

2. Open the tin and place a small piece of paper overlapping the front bottom rim. This is to prevent the knob from adhering to the bottom rim. To make the knob, flatten some Robin's Egg clay; press a tiny ball of Lagoon clay to the center ***(Fig. 9)***. Dab a small amount of Bake & Bond to the upper rim and press the knob to the rim, overlapping the bottom. Follow the manufacturer's instructions to bake the tin; allow to cool.

Fig. 9

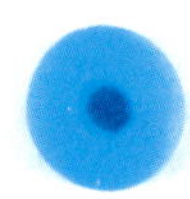

3. Beginning with the most coarse Wet/Dry sandpaper and working to the finest sandpaper, sand the top of the tin. Buff the top of the tin with a soft cloth.

GENERAL INSTRUCTIONS

Basic Tools and Supplies

It is best to use clay dedicated tools. You may not need every tool for each project.

You will need some basic tools. These are the tools you use in almost any project. We suggest the following:

- Sculpey® Clay Conditioning Machine
- Sculpey® Acrylic Roller
- Sculpey® Clay Tool Starter Set
- Sculpey® Super Slicer Set
- wax paper or aluminum foil to protect the work surface
- glass baking dish, metal pan, or cookie sheet covered with an index card for small projects or parchment paper or aluminum foil for large projects

Safety Tips

- Both raw and baked Sculpey is completely safe.
- Do not ingest clay.
- Do not make items which will be used to contain food.
- Bake in a well-ventilated area.

Work Surface

Polymer clay may stain. CLAY MAY DAMAGE UNPROTECTED FURNITURE OR FINISHED SURFACES. DO NOT USE polymer clay on unprotected surfaces.

- Begin with a clean work surface and clean hands. We recommend working on wax paper or aluminum foil. It will be helpful to tape the wax paper or aluminum foil to the work surface. You can also work on a clay dedicated metal baking sheet or Sculpey® Work 'n Bake Clay Mat.

Conditioning Clay

Always wash hands before and after handling clay and between colors.

- Always work with the clay from the lightest color to the darkest color.
- To hand condition the clay, cut the clay into small pieces. Roll the clay into a ball, roll the ball into a log; re-roll the log into a ball and then into a log again. Repeat until all the clay is soft and pliable.

- To condition the clay using the Sculpey® Clay Conditioning Machine, cut the clay into small pieces. Roll the clay with the acrylic roller to make a pancake approximately 1/4" thick. Refer to the manufacturer's instructions to set-up the machine. Run the clay through the machine on the #1 setting until it is soft and pliable. To prevent the colors mixing, wipe the machine between colors.

Rolling Clay Sheets

Clay sheets can be rolled with an acrylic roller or using a clay conditioning machine. Refer to the project instructions for the thickness needed for that project.

- Slightly flatten a conditioned clay ball between your palms to make a pancake.
- To roll sheets with an acrylic roller, place 2 dowels (the diameter of the desired clay sheet thickness) on either side of the pancake. *(**Note:** Using dowels as guides when rolling sheets will keep the thickness of the clay consistent.)*
- With the roller riding on the dowels, roll over the clay until it is flattened.
- To roll sheets using the Sculpey® Clay Conditioning Machine, refer to the manufacturer's instructions.
- If the clay becomes too soft or sticky, place it in a cool area until it firms up and loses the stickiness.

Baking Clay

Do not use a microwave oven. Never exceed the recommended oven temperature or baking time.

- Follow the manufacturer's instructions for baking temperature. For best results, check temperature with an oven thermometer.
- For baking, use a glass baking dish, metal pan, or cookie sheet covered with an index card for small projects or parchment paper or aluminum foil for large projects.
- Baking times vary for different types of clay. Follow the manufacturer's instructions for baking time. Baking should be completed by an adult.

Production Team: Technical Writer – Lisa Lancaster; Technical Associate – Mary Sullivan Hutcheson; Editorial Writer – Susan Frantz Wiles; Senior Graphic Artist – Lora Puls Graphic Artist – Sharvil Salve; Photostylist – Lori Wenger; Photographers – Jason Masters and Ken West.